ZIMMY

THE HUMAN FISH

by
David A. Adler

illustrated by
Rob Shepperson

HOLIDAY HOUSE  NEW YORK

The year 1893 was a year of happy beginnings. People in Chicago rode the first Ferris wheel. Cracker Jacks, the popular candy-coated popcorn, was first made and sold. Juicy Fruit and spearmint gum were introduced by the Wrigley Company. The "Happy Birthday" song was written by sisters Mildred and Patty Hill. And on May 1, 1893, Charles Zibelman, later known as Zimmy, was born in St. Petersburg, Russia. He had a sister named Bertha.

The 1890s were not an easy time for the Zibelmans. There were anti-Jewish riots, known as pogroms, in Russia. Jews were robbed and forced from their homes and jobs. Many were killed. Zimmy's family and thousands of others left for the United States. The Zibelmans moved to Chicago, Illinois.

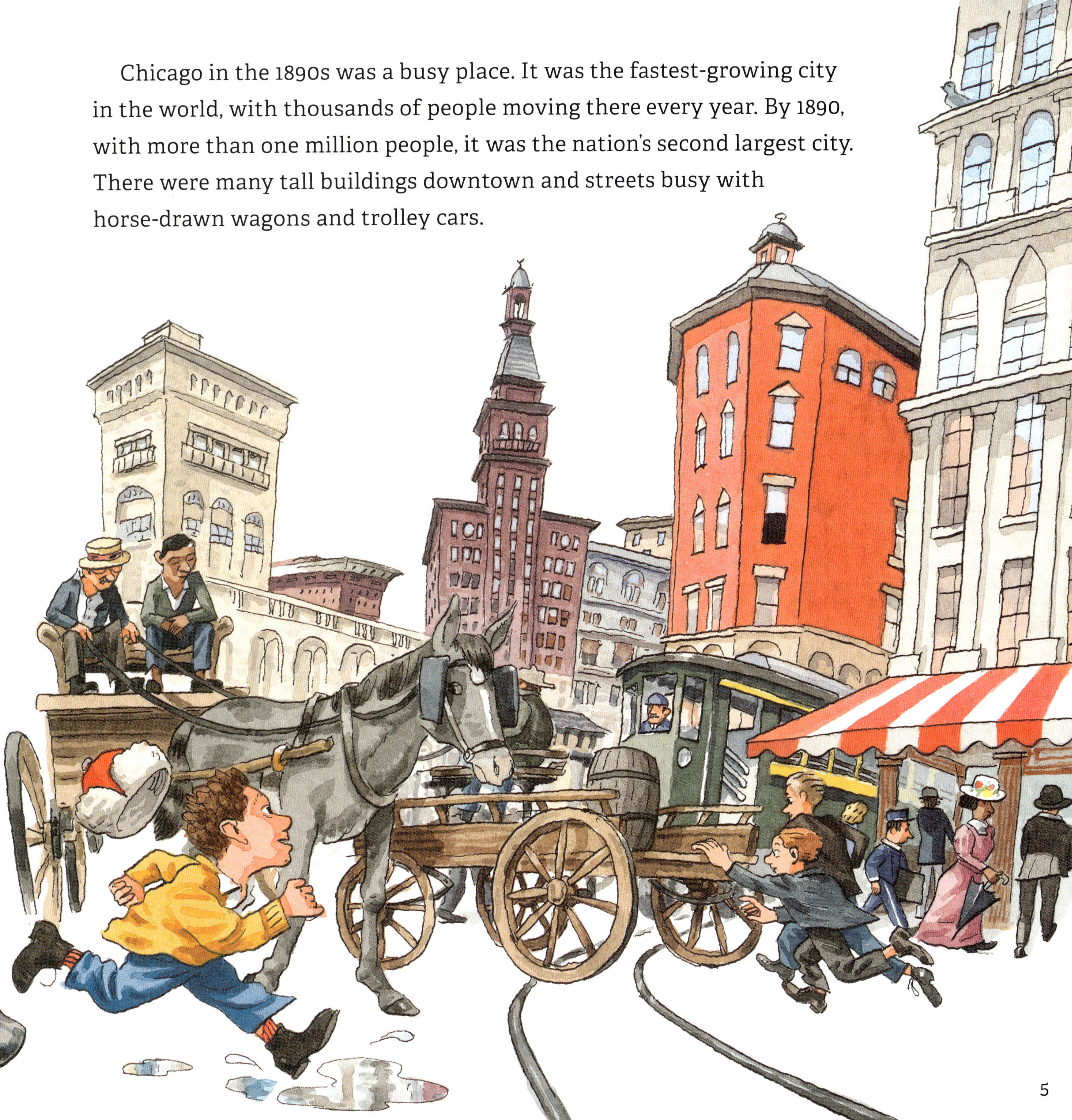

Chicago in the 1890s was a busy place. It was the fastest-growing city in the world, with thousands of people moving there every year. By 1890, with more than one million people, it was the nation's second largest city. There were many tall buildings downtown and streets busy with horse-drawn wagons and trolley cars.

Young Charles Zibelman was busy, too. He was a "newsie" standing on street corners and calling out the day's headlines to sell newspapers. After he sold his armload of papers, he would go back for more. One morning in 1902, nine-year-old Charles was in a hurry to get more papers and hopped on a trolley, but not inside the car. He held on to the side to save the fare. The trolley made a sharp turn that threw Charles off. He fell just as another trolley came by. It ran over the boy and crushed his legs. He was taken to a nearby hospital where doctors amputated his legs. He was left with two small stumps just below his hips.

The tragic accident changed Zibelman but did not defeat him. He attached a roller skate to a board, got on it, and used his arms to push himself around. When he was older, he drove a car especially adapted for someone without legs. And he found he could swim. He claimed that without legs, he had extra buoyancy. He could bounce in the water "like a cork."

To support himself, he gave swimming demonstrations.

In December 1909, sixteen-year-old Charles Zibelman put on a swimming show in a reform school for troubled boys. He lectured and advised the boys to be good, not to smoke or steal, to mind their elders, and to stay away from bad company. He did not always heed his own advice. For most of his adult life, he smoked cigars, sometimes even while he swam.

Throughout the 1920s, he performed in carnivals doing swimming and diving shows. He no longer called himself Charles Zibelman. He called himself Zimmy. In promotions for his act, he was "Zimmy, the Legless Wonder," "Zimmy, the Human Fish," and "Zimmy, the Human Submarine."

In 1931, he traveled to Australia to compete in the Manly International Endurance Swimming Contest. Sixty swimmers, men and women from the United States, England, Italy, New Zealand, and Australia, competed. Mercedes Gleitze won. She was able to keep swimming for more than two days.

In March 1931, in another endurance contest in Sydney, Australia, Zimmy swam for more than fifty hours, beating Gleitze's record. But he didn't win the contest. Frank Roberts, a one-legged Australian, swam even longer.

Four months later in July 1931, Zimmy took on another swimming challenge to beat the endurance record of Otto Kemmerich, a famous German swimmer. In 1928, Kemmerich bet he could continue swimming longer than Leo, his pet sea lion. They swam in an indoor pool in Berlin, Germany. After forty-two hours, the sea lion was too weak to go on. Kemmerich kept going for another four hours.

The new endurance record did not impress Zimmy's manager, Marvin Welt. "A sea lion is nothing," Welt said. "A fish, yes, but Zimmy might even outswim a fish."

In July 1931 in a pool in Honolulu, Hawaii, Zimmy swam for one hundred continuous hours for a new record. But swims in indoor pools did not excite people. Open water swims did.

A few years earlier, in August 1926, Gertrude Ederle swam the rough water between France and England, the English Channel. She was the sixth person and first woman to complete the swim, and she did it in record time. There were front-page newspaper headlines across the world. She returned to New York City to a huge parade along lower Broadway with some two million people cheering for her.

Twenty days later, Otto Kemmerich tried to beat Ederle's record but failed.

Between September 1932 and September 1933, Zimmy made three attempts to swim the Channel but could not complete the swim, once because he was stung by a jellyfish.

It was time for Zimmy to go home.

Sometime before he had gone abroad, probably in the late 1920s, Zimmy married Rose McCullough, a woman who was six years younger and born in England. Later, he married Sally Levine. Zimmy had a son and daughter, both probably with his first wife. Upon his return to the United States, he lived alone in an apartment in New York City.

Audiences for his swim shows were now small. He thought Americans had forgotten him. He felt he needed to do something dramatic. He hoped a swim in the Hudson River from Albany to the new George Washington Bridge in New York City, a distance of about 145 miles, would excite people.

He began the swim on the evening of Monday, August 23, 1937. Two boys coated his body with grease to keep him warm. For his safety, a boat followed him with food, water, and six Red Cross life savers. He lit a cigar. He had told a reporter that for the swim, cigars were as important to him as goggles.

With the cigar in his mouth, he jumped off a pier and into the river, losing his cigar. That didn't worry Zimmy. He had a reported two hundred cigars aboard the boat.

For the endurance swim record, Zimmy didn't have to be constantly swimming. He could rest, but he could not leave the water. Without legs to pull him down, there was little chance of sinking. His disability made it easy for him to sleep in the water. He simply lay back, rested with his folded hands across his chest, and closed his eyes. Sometimes to relax before he fell asleep, he smoked a cigar. He smoked an estimated 150 cigars during the swim.

On the second day, Tuesday, Zimmy rested in a protected cove just off Old Rattlesnake Island. He was waiting for a strong tide that would have pulled him the wrong way to let up. He floated on his back, smoked cigars, and talked with people in boats and along the river's edge. The tide turned, and he swam on.

He soon reached Coxsackie, about twenty-five miles from his starting point. Friends of his were there along the riverbank. They thought he was going too slowly to be able to finish. They urged him to give up.

"No!" Zimmy shouted. "I'm going right on to the George Washington Bridge."

On Wednesday morning, Zimmy came to Saugerties, about forty-eight miles south of Albany. Then a strong tide pushed him six miles north, the wrong way. When the tide let up, he continued the swim and at nightfall reached Saugerties for the second time.

That was the pattern of the swim. In the mornings he swam downstream toward New York City. Then, the afternoon tide took him upstream. He learned to find a protected cove to rest whenever a strong tide worked against him. He rested in the water, ate brandy-soaked sugar cubes and steak sandwiches, and smoked.

As he swam down the Hudson, people along the river's edge and in boats cheered. Some even jumped in the water and joined him for a bit. When they asked how he felt, he said fine—"Fit as a fiddle."

Late on Thursday, he came to the Mid-Hudson Bridge, the halfway mark between Albany and New York. A reporter in a boat got close for an interview. They were near Poughkeepsie, a short distance from Hyde Park where President Franklin Roosevelt had his home. Zimmy told the reporter to tell the president, "I salute you from the waters of the Hudson."

By Thursday at midnight, he had been in the water for 102 straight hours. That beat the previous record of one hundred hours that he had set in Honolulu, Hawaii. Zimmy's hands were cut and sore from being in water so long. He had an upset stomach, but he was eager to go on.

On Saturday, he reached Rockland Landing in Nyack, twenty-nine miles from New York City.

"What's twenty-nine miles?" Zimmy called from the water. "I'm getting near home now, and pretty soon, I'll be there."

By Sunday night, he swam under the George Washington Bridge, a short way from his planned endpoint, the 125th Street Ferry dock. But he couldn't stop. The tide was strong and pulled him for another twenty-seven city blocks, more than a mile downriver.

Rescuers in a rowboat pulled Zimmy from the water. They rowed with him to a dock at 129th Street where an ambulance was waiting to take him to nearby Harlem Hospital. After his almost week-long ordeal, doctors would check his health. He was also expected to rest. But not yet!

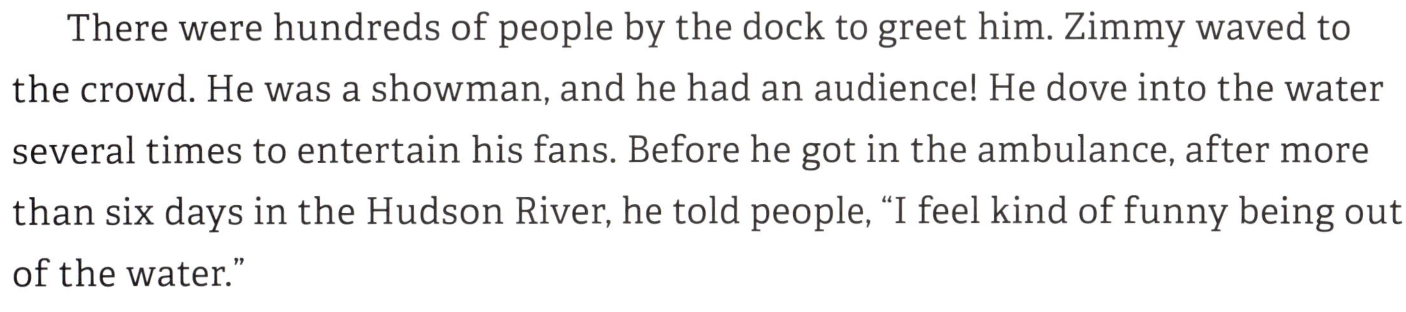

There were hundreds of people by the dock to greet him. Zimmy waved to the crowd. He was a showman, and he had an audience! He dove into the water several times to entertain his fans. Before he got in the ambulance, after more than six days in the Hudson River, he told people, “I feel kind of funny being out of the water.”

He had been in the Hudson River for 147 hours and 37 minutes and swam about 145 miles. “Zimmy’s record,” according to a newspaper report, “probably will stand as a unique accomplishment.”

It was late at night when he arrived at Harlem Hospital. He had lost twenty-six pounds and had a temperature of one hundred, a few degrees above normal. His lungs were congested. The doctors wanted Zimmy to stay and rest.

Zimmy refused. He was already planning his next swim. This one would be from Key West, Florida, to Havana, Cuba. When marathon swimmer Lottie Moore Schoemmel heard his plan, she told reporters that barracudas and other predatory fish would keep Zimmy from making it. He disagreed. "I've got grease I use that I think will keep those fish away."

Zimmy didn't make that swim. It wasn't the danger that stopped him. It was the cost. He would need a boat to shadow him with lifesavers, doctors, and an expert gunman to shoot any sharks that might threaten him. Zimmy didn't have the money for all that. There had been no prize for swimming the Hudson.

ZIMMY'S
Drink like a FISH

To support himself and his family, he performed again in carnivals. To keep himself in the news, he returned to Hawaii where he stayed in a pool for more than a week and broke his own record for continuous swimming.

He was in his fifties when he retired from marathon swimming and settled with his family in Norfolk, Virginia. At first, he had a hot dog stand, then a bar, and then a delicatessen named Zimmy's.

In early November 1952, at fifty-nine, Zimmy had a stroke. He died a few days later on November 9, 1952.

The 1937 newspaper report that his Hudson River swim would "stand as a unique accomplishment" proved to be true.

Zimmy was unique. He refused to allow his disability to limit him.

SOURCE NOTES

p. 3: Zimmy's date and place of birth were taken from his Social Security record and the 1910 U.S. federal census. According to other sources, he was born in Chicago.

p. 5: That 1890 Chicago was the fastest-growing city in the world is from the University of Chicago. https://www.lib.uchicago.edu/collex/collections/chicago-1890s/.

Library website and www.census.gov/quickfacts/chicagocityillinois. By the 1890s, Chicago was the sixth largest city in the world.

p. 8: According to a 1927 review of one of his shows in the *Mount Vernon Argus*, a local newspaper, Zimmy was described as "happy, full of pep . . . and a good comedian." This was quoted in a 2018 article by David Fiske that appeared in the *New York Almanack*. https://www.newyorkalmanack.com/2018/09/charles-zimmys-1937-swim-from-albany-to-manhattan/.

p. 10: The information on Otto Kemmerich and Leo's swims is from the *New York Times*, April 11, 1928, p. 6.

The details of Zimmy's one-hundred-hour swim in a Hawaiian pool is from *Hawke's Bay Tribune*, volume XXI, issue 191, July 28, 1931, p. 2.

p. 14: Zimmy's dates of birth and death and that his wife's name was Sally are from his tombstone in Forest Lawn Cemetery in Norfolk, Virginia. Her death certificate shows she was born in 1905 and died in 1966. She was buried in the same Virginia cemetery.

According to Zimmy's 1942 Draft Registration Card, his wife's name was Sarah and not Sally, which indicates that Sally was his second wife. The 1920 federal census confirms this as it lists Zimmy's wife as Sarah McCullough who was born in 1899. Zimmy had a son named Julius who was born in January 1919 when Sarah was twenty and Sally was just thirteen.

The construction of the George Washington Bridge began in October 1927. https://www.panynj.gov/bridges-tunnels/en/george-washington-bridge/history.html.

Before it was formally named, it was known as the Hudson River Bridge. It opened for traffic in October 1931, and the first to cross the bridge were two children who started on the New York side and roller-skated across to New Jersey. On land, Zimmy also got around on roller skates.

p. 19: That friends called to Zimmy that he should give up and that he replied, "I'm going right on to the George Washington Bridge" is from www.newyorkalmanack.com/2018/09/charles-zimmys-1937-swim-from-albany-to-manhattan/.

p. 20: Zimmy's difficulties with the strong tides near Saugerties are from a report in the *New York Times*, August 26, 1937, p. 23.

p. 22: That Zimmy said, "What's twenty-nine miles . . . soon I'll be there," is from www.newyorkalmanack.com/2018/09/charles-zimmys-1937-swim-from-albany-to-manhattan/.

p. 25: That Zimmy's record would stand as a unique accomplishment is from the *New York Times*, August 30, 1937, p. 23.

For everyone who swims against the tide—R. S.

Printed and bound in September 2025 at C&C Offset, Shenzhen, China.
The artwork was created with watercolor over pen and ink drawing on watercolor paper.
www.holidayhouse.com
First Edition
1 3 5 7 9 10 8 6 4 2

Library of Congress Cataloging-in-Publication Data

Names: Adler, David A., author. | Shepperson, Rob, illustrator.
Title: Zimmy : the human fish / by David A. Adler ; illustrated by Rob Shepperson.
Description: First edition. | New York, N.Y. : Holiday House, [2025] | Audience: Ages 4–8 | Audience: Grades K–1
Summary: "Swimming over one hundred miles from Albany to New York City—six full days in the water—disabled athlete Charles "Zimmy" Zibelman cites having no legs as the key to his skills"— Provided by publisher.
Identifiers: LCCN 2024011616 | ISBN 9780823455508 (hardcover)
Subjects: LCSH: Zimmy, 1893–1952—Juvenile literature. | Swimmers—Russia (Federation)—Biography—Juvenile literature. | Athletes with disabilities—Russia (Federation)—Biography—Juvenile literature.
Classification: LCC GV838.Z56 A35 2025 | DDC 797.2/1092 [B]—dc23/eng/20250210
LC record available at https://lccn.loc.gov/2024011616

ISBN: 978-0-8234-5550-8 (hardcover)

EU Authorized Representative: HackettFlynn Ltd, 36 Cloch Choirneal, Balrothery, Co. Dublin, K32 C942, Ireland. EU@walkerpublishinggroup.com